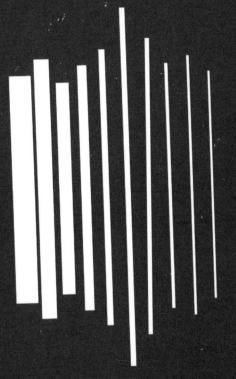

the sinai experiment

Ten Words for God's Chosen People

Ryan Scott

The House Studio, Kansas City, Missouri

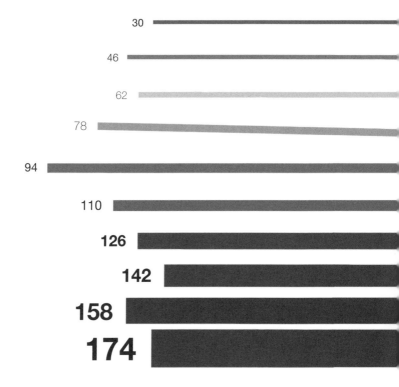

6 the ten words

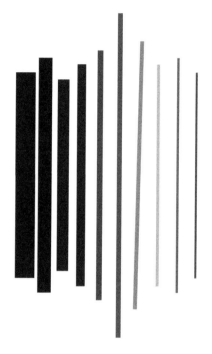

the ten words

The Ten Commandments aren't simply a list of laws or rules. Let's get that out of the way up front. It's no wonder the Hebrews called them the Ten Words. They're so much more than commandments.

If you read *The Kingdom Experiment* from The House Studio, you saw how the Beatitudes were the foundation of the entire Sermon on the Mount and ultimately the framework for teaching the Church how to live in and interact with the world. That foundation was built on this one when, after centuries of slavery, YHWH[1] led a poor, weak people out into the desert. Despite their complaints and persistent failure to listen, God chose these people as an example for the world. In God's design of this world, Israel was to be the model for all other people, showing them how to live as God intended.

These ten words, ten statements, ten commandments allowed the Israelites to see the world from the Creator's perspective. These commandments provided Israel with a foundation to build upon as God's chosen people. Even if the world seemed to show that things worked differently, Israel knew creation worked as God revealed to them.

It's easy for us to go along "knowing" the Ten Commandments without ever taking the time to realize the great insight they possess for our lives. A copy of the Ten Commandments hangs on a wall at the US Supreme

---

[1] God's first name, pronounced "yah-way;" you can read about that in Exodus 3.

Court to symbolize the foundation of law. That might be a bit misplaced though. Simply hanging a list of rules doesn't mean we actually live by them; we should also have these words engraved on our minds to constantly remind us of the foundation for our actions and words.[2]

Back to this book. This is an introduction after all. Most people know what "no killing" and "no lying" mean, so I won't dwell on the obvious points. However, these commandments go much deeper than surface meanings; they became an increasingly vital part of Israelite society and were integrated into every aspect of life. *The Sinai Experiment* explores how the Ten Words should continue to shape the lives of God's people.

We'll also see the ways in which God's people, led by the Spirit, have expanded these commandments. For example, in the time of Moses, a married man committed adultery only if he slept with a married woman; a woman committed adultery if she slept with anyone who wasn't her husband. Today, men have the same responsibilities to their spouses in marriage. This equality, at least where adultery is concerned, is a step in the right direction.

One important note: we may struggle to understand the Old Testament in its proper context, but these sacred words were not challenged by Paul and the Gospels. Quite the opposite. The New Testament is dependent upon these Hebrew Scriptures. Occasionally, I've detoured from the Old Testament in order to note how Jesus built upon the Ten Commandments in his teaching—please don't hold it against me.

The experiments in this book are an attempt to illustrate the ways in which the Ten Words continue to shape our everyday lives. You may not be comfortable with every one of them. You may even disagree with a few of them. That's why this book is designed to be experienced in community. Record your thoughts and share them. Our faith is a communal one; we lean on those around us to help us understand

---

[2] Many Jews still do just that—look up *phylacteries* some time.

what it means to be a Christian. The Ten Commandments have been a centering force for God's people since the beginning. My hope is that they continue to serve that function for us.

and God spoke all these words:

"I am the LORD your God, who brought you out of Egypt, out of the land of slavery.

"You shall have no other gods before me.

"You shall not make for yourself an image in the form of anything in heaven above or on the earth beneath or in the waters below. You shall not bow down to them or worship them; for I, the LORD your God, am a jealous God, punishing the children for the sin of the parents to the third and fourth generation of those who hate me, but showing love to a thousand generations of those who love me and keep my commandments.

"You shall not misuse the name of the LORD your God, for the LORD will not hold anyone guiltless who misuses his name.

"Remember the Sabbath day by keeping it holy. Six days you shall labor and do all your work, but the seventh day is a sabbath to the LORD your God. On it you shall not do any work, neither you, nor your son or daughter, nor your male or female servant, nor your animals, nor any foreigner residing in your towns. For in six days the LORD made the heavens and the earth, the sea, and all that is in them, but he rested on the seventh day. Therefore the LORD blessed the Sabbath day and made it holy.

"Honor your father and your mother, so that you may live long in the land the LORD your God is giving you.

"You shall not murder.

"You shall not commit adultery.

"You shall not steal.

"You shall not give false testimony against your neighbor.

"You shall not covet your neighbor's house. You shall not covet your neighbor's wife, or his male or female servant, his ox or donkey, or anything that belongs to your neighbor."

Exodus 20:1-17

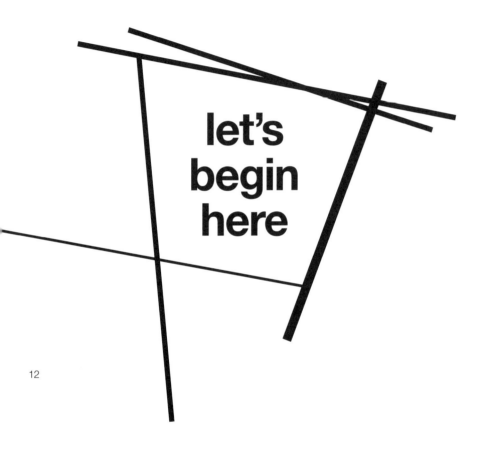

let's begin here

We know you hate directions. But you can always tear out this page and find your own way through the book.

it's plain and simple.

1 Read and discuss a chapter.

2 Each person choose one of six experiments to carry out . . . or make up some of your own.

3 Journal your thoughts on our pages. (Why else would we give you so much white space?)

4 Share your stories with the group next week.

I Am the LORD Your God

A Ten Commandments book with eleven chapters? What gives? Well, the Ten Commandments you learned as a child may differ from the ones your friends know, depending on whether you grew up Protestant, Catholic, or Jewish. I've included every commandment you're familiar with, but the Jews consider this line the first commandment—and a very important one. I don't think they're wrong:

I am the LORD your God, who brought you out of Egypt, out of the land of slavery.

You weren't saved when you asked Jesus into your heart. You were saved when Jesus Christ died on the cross and was raised again. God has already done the saving. Our part is choosing to accept God's loving action and responding with a life of obedience. That's what you did when you prayed; it's what Christians do every day.

Circumstances were no different for Israel. The saving had already been done. God had led them out of Egypt. They had witnessed Pharaoh's army drown in the Red Sea. Their choice was accepting that a God who did all that really did have their best interests in mind. But not just their best interests; God was focused on showing the whole world how best to live in God's creation.

God brought Israel out of Egypt and four centuries of slavery, forming a ragtag bunch of grumbling slaves into a people. God used Israel as an example—their lives showed the world how well things went when they listened to God and how horrible things could get when they didn't. But this commandment isn't about reward and punishment. It's about teaching God's people the best way to live in the world. It's about showing everyone in all time that God is intimately involved with humanity.

One thing it's not about? Power. God didn't send down stone tablets with oppressive laws to show how much bigger and more powerful God is than us. Everything God does is out of love. God loves the world, so we've been given the task of managing what God created. God loves us, so we've been given instructions on how to live well. God is invested in this relationship with creation and is faithful to provide all we need to do our part as a response to God's love.

Living out these commandments requires trust in God and relationship with God. What does it mean for the LORD to be your God?

A covenant is not a one-sided arrangement—relationships are interactive. Do we owe God obedience? Can we repay what God has done for us? Does it even make sense to try?

Engage.

Find a couple you respect (but may not know all that well) who have been married for a number of years. Invite them over to share a meal or coffee with you. Discuss what it means to them to be faithful to each other. Try to go beyond the most obvious definition of faithfulness.

Journal your thoughts here.

19

Observe.

Offer to watch someone's kids for a whole day or a long evening. Think about how from childhood, our actions are determined by rules. How much does a child rely on his or her parents in order to know right and wrong?

Journal your thoughts here.

Listen.

All actions have consequences, both expected and unexpected. Seek out someone who's been in prison. If you're really brave, seek out someone who's still in prison. Ask this person how being incarcerated has affected his or her life.

Journal your thoughts here.

speak.

Tell someone about the difference God's love has made in your life. Choose something specific to share. Choose someone who hasn't heard something like this from you before.

Journal your thoughts here.

25

Reflect.

Pick up a copy of Victor Hugo's novel *Les Misérables.* It's a long book, so feel free to rent the movie instead. Either way, take note of what the work says about sacrifice, selflessness, commitment, and relationship.

Journal your thoughts here.

Serve.

Choose someone you love and see regularly. Spend a day going out of your way to make his or her day better. How difficult is it to constantly put someone else before yourself? How much more difficult would the day have been if this person were not someone special to you?

Journal your thoughts here.

Don't Worship Other Gods

You shall have no other gods before me.

Simple enough, right? It's not like this one is really an issue anymore. At least not for Christians. Ba'al and Molek, even Zeus, Athena, and Aphrodite all "lived" in the past. There's no real danger of us slipping from our faith and turning to them. We have one less commandment to worry about.

But can we actually discount this commandment? A lot of us have fooled ourselves into thinking we can; however, the real test of the gods we serve is in our everyday lives. Do we live as if YHWH is the most important thing? Do our actions reflect God above everything else?

The Israelites were farmers, which means their livelihood depended on rain, and fancy irrigation systems hadn't yet been invented. They also farmed without fertilizer, crop rotation, and all the other revelations of modern farming. All they knew was that rain brought crops, and crops meant they could live a little longer. Their neighbors told them that if they did special rituals at Ba'al's temple, more rain would come. The process seemed to work and their problem seemed insignificant, so they decided not to bother God with it.

For centuries, God's people attempted again and again to solve their own problems. The situation got worse and worse. Eventually, God sent Jesus Christ to physically show people that God really did care about the little things—the poor and the forgotten. Jesus taught, "Look at the birds of the air; they do not sow or reap or store away in barns, and yet your heavenly Father feeds them. Are you not much more valuable than they" (Matt. 6:26)?

Sometimes God seems so big, so mysterious, so distant that it's difficult for us to comprehend just how intimately God is involved in our lives. Just like the Israelites, we fool ourselves into believing that God is only about

31

the big things, that when it comes to the simple problems of everyday life, we're on our own. We get so caught up in the details of living our lives that we forget to live our lives in Christ, to keep God before, above, at the core of everything else. We forget that God is the sole provider of the everyday stuff.

What little things in life do we sometimes think God can't be bothered with? What specifically do we do that shows our lack of trust in God for provision in these areas?

As a people, Israel put other things before God on a regular basis. How does our "Christian" society put things before God? Where do our loyalties lie? How do we make sure our priorities are aligned with God's?

Risk.

A good thing can become harmful if we allow it to come before God: safety and security have become a near-obsession in our society. I'm not encouraging foolishness or unnecessary risks, but...take baby steps. Give a confused-looking stranger the benefit of the doubt. Try leaving the door unlocked while you're at home. Don't lock the door immediately when you get into your car. Whatever you choose, consciously work to assume the best of people rather than the worst.

Journal your thoughts here.

downsize.

Donate one of your favorite wardrobe pieces to a homeless shelter or a charity drive. Don't replace it–just to see if the world really does come crashing down.

Journal your thoughts here.

Sacrifice.

We almost always have more than we need while hundreds of millions of God's people around the world, even some in our towns, go to bed hungry every night. Yet, most of them still wake up the next day. Go light on the meals today. Or go without food altogether in an effort to identify and empathize with those who don't have a choice regarding whether they eat today.

Journal your thoughts here.

38

Provide.

Jesus said the birds of the air depend on God for food and shelter. Sometimes God uses us to provide for others. Check out relationaltithe. com. At the very least, buy a bird feeder—and don't let it sit empty.

Journal your thoughts here.

live.

Sometimes putting God first is as simple as removing the distractions.[3] Spend a day away from TV and the internet; use that time pursuing God's call on your life or continuing to discover what that call is.

Journal your thoughts here.

[3] I got distracted for an hour playing computer games while writing this chapter—it happens to the best of us.

Replace.

When days don't go exactly as we anticipated, so many of us turn to food, exercise, or even friends for comfort—and healthy practices and relationships become our gods. Make yourself aware of those things you turn to rather than God, and consciously work to replace them with God.

Journal your thoughts here.

Don't Replace Me with Images

You shall not make for yourself an image in the form of anything in heaven above or on the earth beneath or in the waters below. You shall not bow down to them or worship them; for I, the LORD your God, am a jealous God, punishing the children for the sin of the parents to the third and fourth generation of those who hate me, but showing love to a thousand generations of those who love me and keep my commandments.

There is some carryover here from the previous commandment. In a world in which no other gods exist, we have only images to substitute in God's place. Like the Israelites who constructed Asherah poles they hoped would provide rain, sometimes we look to the strong nations we have helped create to provide security or an accumulation of wealth and possessions to provide happiness. But these are not the only temptations images provide for us.

Have you ever heard a religious debate in which one person starts his or her argument with, "the God I serve is not like that?" Our perceptions of God differ based on our history, assumptions, culture, doctrine, and experience, but God is so much bigger and more comprehensive than we're able to understand. Although it's only natural that we try to think and speak of God in ways that make sense to us, we run into trouble when we make simplistic images of YHWH and trick ourselves into believing they're the real thing.

Why would God so adamantly command the Israelites to not create images of God? One of the most unique characteristics of YHWH is person-ness. YHWH is a living, active, relational being. God cannot be adequately represented in static form—in wood, stone, or metal. If you read Exodus 32 you see that Israel's sin was not betraying YHWH for another god but creating an image—a golden calf—of YHWH from their perspective. They were making the God they wanted rather than worshipping and obeying the God they had.[4]

[4] We also see God show mercy and set aside the punishment promised in the commandment.

As humans, we long to better know, understand, and relate to a God so big and so mysterious. God has met this longing in Jesus Christ, who is described as the image of the invisible God. YHWH is not encapsulated in bronze or iron, but in a living, breathing human being—One who enters into relationship, loves, hurts, trusts, and forgives.

talk

A snapshot may capture part of a person's character, but it falls short of defining who he or she is. How difficult is it to love and serve a God we can't nail down? Are there some ways we've attempted to simplify God in order to satisfy our own needs?

What images of God (both positive and negative) are espoused by Christians today? How are these accurate depictions of YHWH as revealed in Jesus Christ? How are they inaccurate or incomplete?

Explore.

Attend a Christian worship service at a church whose perspective of God differs from what you're used to—Roman Catholic, Greek Orthodox, a service in a language you don't understand, a Pentecostal service. The list goes on. Just go and participate—you don't have to agree or change your belief system. Think about the vastness of God and the simplicity of our understanding.

Journal your thoughts here.

Integrate.

At different times we've all made scripture into an idol. We forget that its purpose is to bring us to God, and we use it to define God for ourselves. Borrow a commentary from a friend or your pastor or check one out from the library. Read it along with scripture this week. (A good commentary gives background information and a wide variety of interpretations.) How does this background affect the way you understand? How do these different perspectives illustrate the depth of God's communication?

Journal your thoughts here.

consider.

Find a Christian who votes differently from you on some issue. Ask them why. Don't rebut, respond, or react. Ask why and think about what they say.

Journal your thoughts here.

Celebrate.

Participate in the sacrament of communion this week. Remember that we are the body of Christ, quite literally at times. Communion is the act by which God draws us into that body; a diverse conglomeration of Christians are united in Christ through this act. It is the closest we come to seeing an accurate picture of God. How's that for mind blowing?

Journal your thoughts here.

compare.

Visit an art gallery with medieval paintings. If you don't have one nearby, Google some images or better yet, ask a group of children to draw pictures of God. While we want to avoid worshipping one image of God, it is often helpful to see the varying perspectives we have of God. If the artists are available for comment, ask why they drew what they did.

Journal your thoughts here.

Equalize.

Spend the week asking God to reveal parts of God's character you'd prefer to avoid. Pray for God to reveal these things to you. If you embrace the grace of God, pray to see justice; if you find comfort in the omnipotence of God, seek out those times God allows us to decide for ourselves.

Journal your thoughts here.

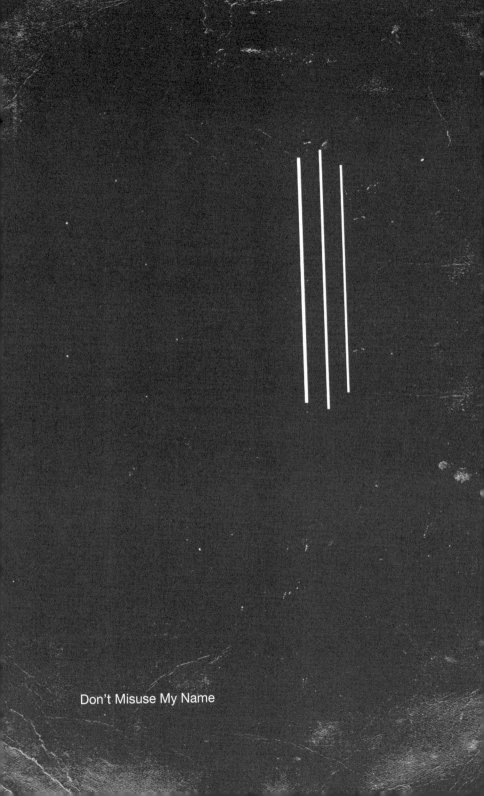

Don't Misuse My Name

You shall not misuse the name of the LORD your God, for the LORD will not hold anyone guiltless who misuses his name.

God is interested in making the name YHWH known. It's the whole point of Exodus—God calling together a people to represent God to the rest of the world. And unlike your typical reality TV star, God cares about the way in which this name is known. The difference, of course, is that God wants to be represented accurately.

But this commandment isn't just about reputation. Knowing God is crucial to getting along well in the world. It matters, with great specificity, the ideas and images conjured in the minds of people when they hear the name of God. There is a particular message to be conveyed. YHWH must mean more than just those beliefs and practices people wish to reject.

When a prominent Christian leader claims natural disasters are punishment for sin, God's name is placed where it doesn't belong. When we say "no good Christian would vote for a Republican (or a Democrat)," we make statements on God's behalf we have no right to make. When a pastor preaches that God's word promises monetary blessings for those who obey, this commandment is violated. These statements and others like them unduly mar the name of God for many who may not already know God.

But this commandment is also about more than just what not to say. Christians have gotten caught up in not using profanity. That's not a bad thing; God's people should avoid coarse speech and offensive words. It is, however, a bit off track. Proper representation of God's name is about more than the words we use but also the sentences and ideas those words combine to form.

Israel carried God's name with them. Now, God's name is literally a part of Christians' identification. The words and actions we take are as important as those we avoid. We can't just tell people what God is not; we must stand up for God's reputation—and even silence can be misuse.

When God's name is misused, do we confront the misuse and with grace, proclaim the truth? Jesus did this in Matthew 5; we can do the same thing. We don't need to be formally-trained theologians or scholars—we need only to reflect our relationship with God and speak from the heart.

In what ways have you heard God's name misused? How can we speak out for our beliefs without misrepresenting God?

In what ways have you been negligent in speaking out for God? How can we help each other overcome our fears of being different from the rest of the world?

repent.

For all the good we've done, Christians have also done our share of misrepresenting God—and hurting people in the process. Apologize to someone, maybe a complete stranger, for Christians' inappropriate or unloving misuses of God's name. If you can't think of a particular person, group or misuse, go to Google; "Christian hypocrisy" might be a good place to start.

Journal your thoughts here.

Witness.

Stand on a busy corner with a sign that reads, "God is love." Dress well and talk to people. Please don't take their money.

Journal your thoughts here.

Mingle.

God is not represented well when divisions exist among Christians. Find a way to bridge gaps. Whether you do this simply by taking the pastor of another local congregation out to lunch or by working with all the Christian congregations in town to publish a joint statement in the newspaper, do something to actively participate in the unity that exists because of our belief and trust in Christ.

Journal your thoughts here.

70

offend.

Although we shouldn't choose offensive words, the subject of our words might offend a few people from time to time. Speak out against materialism or celebrity culture. Make a conversation slightly uncomfortable. Mention a few people who embody the name of God with their lives. Better yet, mention the God who empowers them.

Journal your thoughts here.

Nourish.

Take a hot meal to a homeless person. Spend time with a lonely nursing home resident. Show and tell (no, this isn't a reference to kindergarten take-your-teddy-bear-to-school day) someone who's often forgotten or overlooked that they mean something to you and to God. Do it more than just this one time.

Journal your thoughts here.

Flashback.

Pay attention to your words. Mom's not around to wash your mouth out with soap; you'll have to make up your own mind about what to say. Partner with someone—a friend, spouse, roommate, co-worker—and keep yourselves accountable for the ways you speak about God.

Journal your thoughts here.

Remember the Sabbath

Remember the Sabbath day by keeping it holy. Six days you shall labor and do all your work, but the seventh day is a sabbath to the LORD your God. On it you shall not do any work, neither you, nor your son or daughter, nor your male or female servant, nor your animals, nor any foreigner residing in your towns. For in six days the LORD made the heavens and the earth, the sea, and all that is in them, but he rested on the seventh day. Therefore the LORD blessed the Sabbath day and made it holy.

Sabbath means rest. This concept was a lot easier to understand when people spent every sunlit hour at manual labor just to survive, wake up the next day, and do it all over again. For farmers, whose crops and animals needed constant attention, taking a whole day off exhibited profound trust in the God who ultimately sustains all life.

So rest and trust—these are our Sabbath lessons. We could write a whole book on the concept of Sabbath. Some have.[5] But the best way to understand Sabbath is to practice Sabbath. Our society has ingrained in us the value of hard work; we're taught to be efficient and diligent. Sometimes we can go overboard. Scripture teaches that God built rest into creation as a vital part of the whole. If you're the kind of person who creates to-do lists, each list should include spending some significant time away from the list.

For most modern Christians the Sabbath has been associated with our day of worship. But for those who have to get the kids dressed and out the door then attend services, Sunday school, a couple of practices, and still make food for the small group, Sunday is anything but restful. Even our worship services try to pack so much into one hour we barely get time to breathe.

You may not be able to change your busy Sunday routine (though you should try, and try hard). But you do need to find some time for Sabbath.

[5] I recommend *Living the Sabbath* by Norman Wirzba.

It's not a time to sit and do nothing. Rest can be a walk in the woods or time to explore your creative outlets. Take photos. Write a poem. Make dinner as a family. Clean up together. The point is to enjoy God and God's creation, to stop and smell the roses (both literally and metaphorically). Sabbath is not laziness; it's productivity of a different kind—it's rest and restoration for another week ahead.

Are our worship services too busy? Do we practice Sabbath in our worship? What could we do to better prepare and enable ourselves to practice Sabbath in our Sabbath worship?

Sabbath is not a principle for only God's people—it is God's intention for all creation. What can you do in your life to share Sabbath with those around you during the week?

Retreat.

Find a monastery nearby and join in worship with the monks (there are usually five times or more a day to choose from). At the very least, show up at church before things get busy. Sit in the sanctuary and think about what it means to rest in God.

Journal your thoughts here.

abstain.

In some denominations it used to be common to avoid spending money on Sundays so no one would have to work on the Sabbath on our account. This practice has the potential to lead to legalism, but try it for a week. It may require more preparation than you expect; it takes effort to experience Sabbath.

Journal your thoughts here.

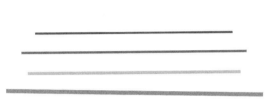

Vacate.

Take a day (or an afternoon) off. At least cancel your post-workday obligations. Get outside. Read a book. Enjoy creation.

Journal your thoughts here.

Unburden.

Bag your own groceries. Return your shopping cart to its rightful location *inside* the grocery store doors. Park your own car. Reshelve the pair of jeans you tried on rather than handing them to the fitting room attendant. Discover the joy of allowing someone else a break.

Journal your thoughts here.

broaden.

Visit a farm. They're fewer in number these days, but many farms have websites and offer tours (real ones—not just virtual views) to visitors. If they welcome volunteer labor, don't leave at the end of the tour; instead, spend a day working alongside them. Get a glimpse into the context of Sabbath.

Journal your thoughts here.

Yield.

Take time off from some of your normal duties at home, work, or church (this includes you, pastors). Let someone else teach Sunday school or unlock the building. Give your new co-worker a chance to make the presentation. Find a way to put into action your trust in God's sustaining hand. Things will still get done. Trust ~~me~~ God.

Journal your thoughts here.

Honor Your Parents...and Other People's Parents

Honor your father and your mother, so that you may live long in the land the LORD your God is giving you.

This isn't about calling your mother more often.[6] I'm sure you're expecting it by now, but this commandment is not quite as simple as it seems. The use of the vague word "honor" is intentional; this command is not to a specific act but to a specific attitude. Whatever actions constitute honoring one's father and mother, it's pretty clear that the respect and care involved should surpass whatever is adequate.

While respect for parents is a valuable trait to teach the young, this command is directed most specifically to adult children. You may have heard cliché stories about elderly Eskimos being set adrift on ice floes when they became a burden for the tribe. I don't know how accurate those stories are, but it was not unheard of for similar practices to take place among the tribes around Israel.

This command is a clear indication from God that all lives are valuable. If honoring our fathers and mothers requires sacrifice from the tribe, we must make that sacrifice, and make it happily. Caring for our own parents also creates a pattern of care which we too will enjoy one day. The promise of long life is simply a result of obeying this command.

Today, people live longer, and we have created institutions to help us honor our mothers and fathers as they age. Interestingly, these are the same institutions that enable us to forget more easily the needs of our parents. It's also easier to forget that this command is communal; you are not absolved of responsibility for others if your own parents have passed away.

Again we're forced to think a little more about what exactly God is asking us to do. This is not an easy commandment. It is easy for us to push aside or exclude those who most need to be included. Our lives are hard

---

[6] But please, call your mother.

enough without adding relationships that require extra effort. The elderly, the sick, the handicapped, the orphaned—caring for them just has to be someone else's responsibility.

But what would happen if God took that attitude toward us?

talk

The word honor probably means something more than adequate physical care. Do our mothers and fathers (not just our biological parents) continue to be a part of our lives, our congregation's life?

If this command is really about the care of those who, at times, need extra help or attention, what considerations should we make for those with handicaps and disabilities — whether elderly or not? How well do we do this now?

Plan.

If you have children, help make this commandment a little easier for them. Put together a living will and talk it over with them. If you don't yet have children, honor your parents by creating your own living will and discussing it with them. Although no parent wants to bury a child, if anything should happen, they'll be aware of your wishes.

Journal your thoughts here.

Substitute.

Seek out parents whose children live far away. Invite them to dinner or to your kids', nieces' or nephews', or friends' children's sports or music events. Include them in your life. Even the most active, involved people need a sense of family.

Journal your thoughts here.

write.

Reflect on all your parents have done for you. Write—don't type—a letter to them (they have this crazy thing now called a pen). Tell them how you feel. If your parents are no longer around, share the letter with your kids, siblings, or any other family members you're close to. If your parents have never been there, write to someone who's been a mother or father to you.

Journal your thoughts here.

Volunteer.

Many retirement homes, especially those for veterans or the poor, are understaffed and overcrowded. Find one near you and offer some time to work in any way they might need you.

Journal your thoughts here.

Advocate.

One of the reasons some congregations have no handicapped or disabled members is because something makes it difficult for them to fully participate. Do some research. What changes might be necessary to fully welcome all people to worship with you?

Journal your thoughts here.

gather.

Most congregations have members who cannot get to worship due to illness or mobility. Get some friends together and bring the service to them. Spend your Sunday morning worshipping together.

Journal your thoughts here.

Don't Murder

You shall not murder.

Actually, the word in Hebrew is "kill," and it's used in a variety of ways in Hebrew Scriptures—from accidental death to capital punishment to violence with intent to kill. The translators chose the word murder here as a way to avoid disagreements over interpretation, but even if we argue over which word to use and what it means, we still often overlook a deeper discussion.

Humans have no right to kill on their own authority. Only God has the right to take life. This is a fundamental tenet of the creation story. We see that God's choices to take life have all involved violations of how God ordered creation. Israel had death penalties for offenses like dishonoring one's parents or breaking the Sabbath—acts we consider "lesser" crimes. For Israel these were direct violations of the way creation was intended to function.

This makes it imperative for us to view killing in a different light. In an age when our methods of killing can devastate all of creation and have long-lasting effects on future generations, we have to ask different questions about the appropriateness of their use. We also have to take seriously the words of Jesus in Matthew 5, in which he extends the command against murder to include anger and broken relationships. Throughout the Bible, reconciliation is the primary aim of human action. Even in killing, reconciliation must be the end result.

But that still doesn't give us an answer. Clearly killing is not good or desirable; there is a commandment against it. Yet we see passages in which killing is part of restoring God's created order. The debate has raged, most likely from the moment Moses brought these tablets down from the mountain, and it continues to crop up because it's that important; the one thing we must absolutely avoid is settling the matter and leaving the discussions behind.

War, capital punishment, euthanasia, suicide, self-defense, abortion—all of these difficult issues involve our understanding of killing. As much as we'd like to separate them from each other, we must never deny their interconnection. The Christian faith is one that affirms life; we believe all life is valuable because Christ died for all. Yet we live in an imperfect world. We're supposed to struggle with killing. The taking of life should be the rarest of human action, something done without anger, arrogance, or vengeance, and certainly without pleasure.

talk

How do we create space to allow discussions on killing to take place without conversations being overrun by emotion and the personal connection so many have to this topic?

Does this chapter change the way you view anger, forgiveness, and love of enemies? What does it mean for reconciliation to be the motivating factor for all our actions? Is this something we can even do?

pray.

There are situations in which even those of us most fervently opposed to killing reluctantly admit that ending the life of another may be justified. It is difficult enough to make that realization in theory. Spend time in prayer for those who must act on that conclusion. Pray for grace in the midst of sorrow. Pray for reconciliation.

Journal your thoughts here.

Mourn.

Attend a portion of a murder trial or the sentencing of someone who has already been found guilty of murder. Do it respectfully and responsibly. Witness the real results of lost life—grief, anger, sorrow, confusion, hopelessness. Every life is sacred; there are no faceless deaths. Pray for both the murdered and the murderer.

Journal your thoughts here.

Rejoice.

This commandment is as much about understanding the value of life as it is about violence or anger. A great way to honor and appreciate life is to celebrate it. Take some kids bowling. Play cards at the senior center. Invite the neighbors over for a cookout. Throw a party for no other reason than to enjoy life.

Journal your thoughts here.

mediate.

Look up information on Victim-Offender Reconciliation Programs (VORP).
These groups work to bring healing and reconciliation to hurting people
while respecting the life and humanity of everyone involved. Find a group
in your area and participate.

Journal your thoughts here.

Support.

At times, soldiers are asked to do unimaginable, unspeakable acts. Whether we're warriors or rabidly nonviolent, we all must have compassion for those dealing with the difficult experiences of life and death. Send a letter to a combat veteran (military or otherwise); let them know you're praying. We can't all be counselors, but we can be strength and support to those in need.

Journal your thoughts here.

Discover.

The world is far more interconnected than we'd like to believe. Watch the movie *Blood Diamond* or research the African diamond trade. Think about how your own actions can contribute to killing in other parts of the world.

Journal your thoughts here.

Don't Commit Adultery

You shall not commit adultery.

Marriage was instituted by God and symbolizes the faithful commitment between God and God's chosen people: the expectations of that covenant extend to marriage as well. Husbands and wives exemplify to each other the love God shows to all of us. Humans were created as relational beings; we need each other. Marriage and family are a built-in support system for faithful living. Violating the trust required in these relationships is an affront to God's character and God's design for creation.

This commandment is not one to take lightly. Adultery was punishable by death even in Jesus's time and beyond. Jesus expanded the scope of adultery, saying, "Anyone who looks at a woman lustfully has already committed adultery with her in his heart" (Matthew 5:28). Adultery is essentially depersonalizing someone else. From treating a man as no more than the sum of his body parts to participating in a selfish, fleeting gratification of physical or emotional desires, adultery is action that drives people apart. It works against God's desire for unity and the reconciliation of all people.

And since marriage is such an important part of Christian life, it's not a private matter. Too often we expect couples to deal with their relationships behind closed doors, or we speak in whispers about difficulties as if struggles in marriage are a rarity. But in the Church, marriage is everyone's business; no man or woman can fulfill the duties and responsibilities of marriage without the support of a loving community.

We can't discuss adultery without addressing sex. Monogamy contradicts the biological drives of our bodies. Yet with sex, as with every other human desire, we recognize the long-term value of discipline over immediate gratification. Only in a committed marriage can people fully express their sexuality. Without trust in the faithfulness of a spouse, we are always holding something back.

And our understanding of adultery, monogamy, and sex affects more than just husband and wife. Children learn about God's love through the way their parents treat each other. Those who are not married develop healthy relationships through positive examples. God has given marriage as a means of teaching honor, integrity and fidelity to all people. Life as God intends it depends on us taking marriage seriously.

talk

What barriers prevent marriage from becoming a community matter? How can we surpass these barriers in healthy and beneficial ways?

Have you ever thought about adultery as the depersonalization of another human? Does using this definition change the way you view your relationships, both inside and outside the context of marriage?

Intrude.

Ask a married friend about his or her relationship. Start a discussion about fidelity—both emotional and physical. Share your own struggles and successes. If you don't know anyone well enough to have this conversation, begin to cultivate a friendship; hopefully you'll be able to ask these questions at some point in the future.

Journal your thoughts here.

vow.

For all you married people—write a letter to your spouse. Tell him or her the things you might have said at your wedding if you had known then what you know now. Read it aloud so he or she can hear your words.

Journal your thoughts here.

Commit.

Real Sex by Lauren Winner is a book about Christian relationships and chastity; it's a good resource for all people—married or single. Read it. Make some commitments to God. Share them with a friend who can help you keep them.

Journal your thoughts here.

Examine.

Take inventory of your viewing habits—your DVD collection, your TV schedule, and so on. How many of them depersonalize someone? If you're not sure, check with your spouse or a friend whose perspective differs from yours.

Journal your thoughts here.

represent.

A lot of people have no example of a committed, loving marriage in their lives. If you're married, invite someone into your life this week (and hopefully for the long term). Don't worry about being on your best behavior. Just be yourselves. If you aren't married, ask a married couple if they'll give you a glimpse into their life together.

Journal your thoughts here.

Discuss.

Speak with your parents or other family members about marriage and relationships—even if their relationships aren't happy ones. Our family members want the best for us and have more experience than we'd like to admit sometimes. Listen to what they have to say. Ask questions.

Journal your thoughts here.

Don't Steal

You shall not steal.

Don't take things that belong to other people, and don't stand by when someone else does. You probably learned this principle when you were five or so, and hopefully by now it's sunk in pretty well. The problem is, when it comes to stealing, we've developed a very narrow focus.

Israel understood creation as a whole—something interconnected and something of which they were only a part. They knew that human beings were created in God's image and were entrusted to play a special role in the care of the rest of creation (Genesis 2:15, 19-20). Their understanding of creation still applies today. We were given work to do with the expectation that through this work God would provide for our needs. It's not something we do for ourselves; it's the part we play in God's bigger plan.

A thief bypasses this system entirely, showing contempt for God's plan and undermining the humanity of both thief and victim. So then, working hard and reaping rewards become the norm for human action. Disharmony arises when some people receive without working and others work as hard as they can while receiving less than they need to survive. In both these scenarios people are living a life less than human, less than God's intention for them.

Inequality has existed forever, and it seems every generation's politicians have proposed their own fix to the problem. Inequality isn't really the issue though; some will always have more than others. This commandment is about recognizing the humanity of others. When we participate in a system that allows some, both rich and poor, to receive without working, we rob them of some part of their humanity, and, by extension, we rob ourselves.

In a world of international commerce, we rarely see the places or people from which our possessions come. Are those who work to make our things receiving enough to live on? Do they work in conditions that respect their dignity as human beings? Do people even have the opportunity to work at all?

God created us to be a part of the whole, not isolated individuals. We have a responsibility to each other. We can't take something that belongs to other people, and we can't stand by when someone else does—especially when that thing is our own humanity.

talk

Do we really believe creation is interconnected? Do we live as if we understand that our actions affect others? Should we abandon this ancient Hebrew way of understanding the world, or can we learn from this perspective?

Christians have an obligation to care for those who are unable to care for themselves (check out chapter six of this book, or, you know, just about any book of the Bible). We cannot simply ignore the needs of the poor or forcefully take money from the rich. So what options do we have to help return balance to our system of work, reward, and survival?

Work.

Much of the labor we do these days is intellectual. For many of us, our survival is not dependent on our physical abilities, so we are disconnected from the experience of a day of physical work. Find a place to do manual labor, and spend a whole day at it. Experience the fatigue and exhilaration. Does this work give you a new perspective on your humanity?

Journal your thoughts here.

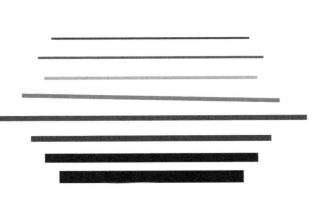

Investigate.

Find out where your food and clothes are produced. Can the farmers and workers live on the wages they're paid? Are some brands better than others at providing for their employees? Read up on responsible clothing production and fair trade goods. If your Google searches aren't fruitful (pun intended), try transfairusa.org or ciw-online.org. Share what you find with your friends and family. Individual choices do have an impact over time.

Journal your thoughts here.

contribute.

Education is the key to improving the lives of the unemployed and underemployed—and their families. Many children grow up in places where subsistence living is all they know. Volunteer your time tutoring or mentoring in a low-income community. Plenty of organizations would love to have your time and effort.

Journal your thoughts here.

Assist.

You can contribute to the education and success of people across the globe. Sponsor a child with ncm.org, compassion.com, or another respected organization. You can make a personal connection with a child and play a major role in enabling them to fulfill their creative purpose. If you can't afford to sponsor a child on your own, ask a friend to join you.

Journal your thoughts here.

Acknowledge.

Do you enjoy your job? Is it engaging? Fulfilling? If so, express your appreciation to the people who are responsible for keeping you employed. Don't just walk by and say thanks. Take the time to think about what this opportunity means to you and your life.

Journal your thoughts here.

furnish.

When Israel received these commandments for the first time, their only understanding of luxury was of the Egyptians they had served as slaves. For them, the prohibition of stealing was all about protecting those things that were necessary for their livelihood and well-being. This is the still the situation for many around the world. Check out heifer.org and give the gift of livestock to people who depend on animals in order to survive. Again, combine your money with a friend if you can't afford this one alone.

Journal your thoughts here.

Don't Lie or Gossip

You shall not give false testimony against your neighbor.

There was no CSI in ancient Israel. There were no surveillance cameras, lab tests, or fingerprint analyses to determine what really happened during the commission of a crime. Instead, the whole system depended on people—both the offender and the offended—telling the truth. Those in the wrong were expected to fess up and make things right; those who challenged a charge laid themselves at the mercy of the community. Giving false statements disrupted the whole order of societal justice.

Israel understood this commandment as a safeguard to personal integrity and as a standard of respectful interaction within the community. God expected the Israelites to treat all people with respect and honor, both in public and in private. God's people have this same responsibility today, which means our polite smiles and handshakes with Mrs. Baxter after Sunday school followed by our complaints at home about her negative attitude violate this commandment.

God granted humans the ability to choose between right and wrong, and we mess up. We fight and argue and challenge each other—sometimes more often than we get along. Human interaction is messy. God understands that. This commandment is insight on how to navigate those challenges. God's people shouldn't slander or insult people; we shouldn't attempt to ruin reputations or make snide comments behind someone's back.

159

No false testimony is a call to be gracefully and respectfully up-front and honest with people. Paul called this kind of honesty "speaking the truth in love" (Ephesians 4:15). God's people should be united; any action we take should be for the building up of the whole body. This is very difficult to do without being in relationship with each other. If we do not know the heart of the people who correct us, it's easy to assume their motives are malicious.

This commandment digs deep at the heart of how we view other people. It uproots our penchant to stereotype and our aversion to intimacy. It shows us time and again that living with integrity is not as easy as we'd like to believe. Yes, this commandment began with a call to respect and honor so legal systems can function properly, but ultimately it reminds us that we should not need a judge or an oath to speak honestly and respect others as the children of God they were created to be.

talk

Matthew 18:15-20 gives us a specific plan for dealing with conflict in the Church. What barriers might we have to overcome in order to use this plan in our churches today? How does the commandment against false testimony figure into the discussion?

What is a white lie? What is the motivation behind telling one? Are there changes to be made in your relationships to make it easier to speak honestly in situations where you might otherwise tell a white lie?

Bolster.

We all know our legal system is less than perfect. (I'm not sure we could have expected more from Israel's.) Nevertheless, our system exists as an attempt to apply some measure of justice in society. Write a letter to a judge or public defender thanking them for their honesty, integrity, and dedication to justice.

Journal your thoughts here.

163

Praise.

If you hear something negative about a person this week, respond with something positive about them. If you don't know this person, help your friend take a step back and think. Try to help your friend find some way for them to express frustration without demeaning or insulting other people.

Journal your thoughts here.

humanize.

Put yourselves in someone else's shoes, especially someone you tend to view as part of a group—"those people" or "people like that." Whether "those people" are Democrats, Republicans, bad drivers, the neighbors, cool kids, or the homeless, think of that group as individuals. What must their life be like? What makes this person act as they do? Respond to these people as people, even if they don't treat you the same way.

Journal your thoughts here.

Grapple.

Derek Webb writes songs with difficult truths that challenge Christians. Find the lyrics to his tune "My Enemies Are Men Like Me;" listen to the song. Think about what you agree with, what challenges you, frustrates you, angers you; don't be surprised if all your answers are the same. Life, as God designed it, is not simple.

Journal your thoughts here.

Champion.

This commandment is rooted in the legal process. In our justice system, money can often be a determining factor for quality representation and fair treatment. Legal aid societies provide legal services for those who cannot afford them. Find one in your area and donate some time or money to support people facing their day in court. As you walk through this experience, think about how important honesty and integrity are to the process.

Journal your thoughts here.

atone.

If a name has not already come to mind, pray for God to reveal someone you've hurt by false testimony. Go to this person and do your part to reconcile the relationship.

Journal your thoughts here.

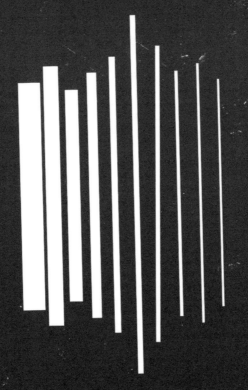

Don't Covet

You shall not covet your neighbor's house. You shall not covet your neighbor's wife, or his male or female servant, his ox or donkey, or anything that belongs to your neighbor.

We all have wants. Things we don't have that we'd like to. We see them on TV, in magazines, as we're driving around in our cars; we're inundated with things we don't have that could be ours. Israel didn't have advertising. Their ideas for something different came when they saw others with those things. So this commandment is not so much about "I wish I had Jim's wife," but "I wish my wife did this the way Jim's wife does." It's the temptation to be discontent.

Throughout this book we've seen how each of the commandments represents boundaries that keep our actions within God's plan for creation. By acting within these boundaries, we avoid upsetting the balance God intended. Our desires are endless. Human selfishness would overrun the world without some measure of discipline. Coveting is the ultimate expression of that selfishness. It's the desire for more and more simply because there is more to be had.

All too often it seems our society is based on this idea of more. We're told to desire increasingly lavish lifestyles. To spend and buy. To accumulate and expand. We leave behind the idea of meeting our needs in favor of satisfying our wants, regardless of how this way of living affects us and the world around us. You need a bigger house because it's a better investment. You have to replace your cell phone after six months because the next version is out. Trendy clothes, luxurious cars, new gadgets. The list goes on.

Hopefully *The Sinai Experiment* has helped you see that human beings are equally valuable no matter what their situation. Our stuff and status have nothing to do with our value as people. As we accumulate more and more, we have more things to take our focus away from God and the life God designed us to lead. It becomes easier to forget what's really important.

We're meant to rely on God, to find our identification in Jesus Christ, whose example was one of a homeless wanderer willing to give everything, even his own life, out of love for humanity. I have a hard time believing Jesus worried at all about what he didn't have.

talk

What would your friends say if you began to cut back, scale down, and save rather than upgrade and spend? What problems might this change create in your social interactions? How would this affect your view of yourself?

What does it mean to be satisfied? Is this different from being content?

Quit.

Turn down something free. Sure, you might find a use for it at some point, but you don't need it. Take this one small step outside the system of more, the society of consumption.

Journal your thoughts here.

Keep.

Hang on to your cell phone until it dies (and no throwing it in the toilet on purpose). If you can still use it to make and receive calls, to send and receive texts, it's doing its job, right? Mine's going on four years—can you beat that? If cell phones aren't your thing, avoid replacing something else—car, computer, iPod, shoes. The possibilities are endless.

Journal your thoughts here.

fast.

Chose something you use every day and go without it—for a day, a week, a month. Discipline in one area of our lives helps us learn discipline in all areas of life. Depending on what you choose, you may never need to use it again.[7]

Journal your thoughts here.

[7] I'm no doctor, but I would recommend you continue to eat on a semi-regular basis.

Join.

Start a sharing club or join an existing group at freecycle.org. Work with your friends or neighbors to share something. Start small, like books or a babysitter. Then go big—like a barbeque grill or a car. There's no need to each have something you may not use very often.

Journal your thoughts here.

Zero.

Wipe the slate clean. Don't keep track of the score. In Luke 6:34, Jesus talks about lending without expecting to get anything back. Instead of asking, let it go. Forget about it. Added bonus: you'll get a pleasant surprise if whatever you lent makes it back to you.

Journal your thoughts here.

extract.

Go through your things—dishes, books, clothes, gadgets. Take everything you can't remember using and give it to someone who needs it. Why should we have nine sets of measuring cups when some people don't have any? Please skip the garage sale—it just encourages the same habits in others you're trying to avoid yourself.

Journal your thoughts here.